What is a butterfly?

 Butterflies and moths belong to the group of insects with scale-covered wings called the Lepidoptera. Lepis means scale and ptera means wings. There are about 20,000 species of butterflies and 147,000 species of moths.

A butterfly's mouth is shaped like a thin straw and can be rolled up and down. It is called a proboscis. When it is hungry, the butterfly unwinds its proboscis and dips it into a flower to feed on the nectar inside. Some butterflies also feed on rotten fruit, or dead animals or from puddles.

Butterflies fly by day and have two pairs of overlapping wings covered in scales. The wings are not hooked together. Most moths fly at night and have wings that are hooked together. Butterflies rest with their wings held together above the body or held out flat. Many moths rest with their wings folded like a tent above their body.

This book belongs to

....

Life-cycle

When you are born you look like a human. When a butterfly is born it doesn't look like a butterfly. First it is an egg, then a caterpillar hatches from the egg, the caterpillar changes into a pupa, and the pupa changes into a butterfly. The butterfly mates and if it is a female it lays eggs and the life cycle starts again. Match the stickers to the correct outlines.

Butterfly eggs may be round, oval or cylindrical. They can be wrinkled and pitted or smooth and polished.

1 The female butterfly lays its eggs on a plant. Each butterfly has a favourite plant, called a host plant.

2 A tiny caterpillar hatches from the egg and starts eating. First it eats its eggshell and then the leaves of the host plant.

3 The caterpillar has a pair of jaws for chewing leaves and a long gut for digesting its food. It eats almost non-stop until it has stored enough nutrients to become a pupa and later a butterfly.

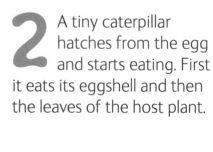

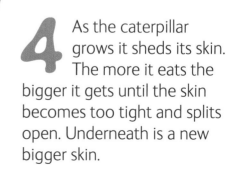

4 As the caterpillar grows it sheds its skin. The more it eats the bigger it gets until the skin becomes too tight and splits open. Underneath is a new bigger skin.

Most caterpillars grow 5 new skins in their life but some only grow 4 and some as many as 9.

5 When it is fully grown, the caterpillar stops feeding and turns into a pupa. Many species make a cocoon, that is like a shelter, to protect the pupa.

6 Inside the pupa the body is changing – the proboscis forms, its legs grow longer, it develops wings and grows new muscles for flight.

7 Eventually the pupa splits open and a butterfly with wings and a drinking straw proboscis emerges.

A fully grown caterpillar can be over 1,000 times heavier than when it first came out of its egg.

8 The butterfly has to wait until its wings are dry and unfolded before it can start flying. It also has to wait for enough oxygen to pass through its tiny veins. Then it looks for something to feed on, like nectar from flowers, and a butterfly to mate with.

Colours and names

The wings of butterflies and moths are covered in thousands of tiny scales. The colours and patterns on the wings are made by the scales. The names of butterflies and moths often include a colour. Stick the butterflies on the correct outlines.

Common name: Orange tiger butterfly
Species name: *Dryadula phaetusa*
Location: Mexico to Brazil

This orange butterfly has black stripes and is poisonous to any animal that tries to eat it.

Common name: Sapphira butterfly
Species name: *Asterope sapphira*
Location: The Amazon in Brazil

This is found in undisturbed forest along river valleys, and flies slowly and perches under leaves.

Common name: Postman butterfly
Species name: *Heliconius melpomeone*
Location: Colombia, Brazil, Bolivia

This butterfly is called the postman because it flies round all the nectar plants where it lives, visiting them one by one, like a postman delivering letters to houses.

Common name: Atlas moth
Species name: *Attacus atlas*
Location: Southeast Asia

The Atlas moth is one of the largest moths in the world. It has patterns on the tips of its wings that look like the head of a snake. Parts of the wings are transparent, so when the moth is resting it looks like a pile of dead leaves.

Common name: Blue mormon butterfly
Species name: *Papilio polymnestor*
Location: Southern India, Sri Lanka, western Java

This black, blue and white butterfly likes feeding on the salts in damp mud. It also sometimes lands on animal droppings to feed on the moisture in them!

Common name: American moon moth
Species name: *Actias luna*
Location: Eastern North America

A beautiful pale green moth with a white woolly body and a purple collar, and tails on its hindwings.

Common name: Plain tiger butterfly
Species name: *Danaus chrysippus*
Location: Africa, Arabia, Australia, Canary Islands, India, Sri Lanka, Burma

The butterfly is orange with black and white marks on it. It is a common butterfly and is poisonous to its predators.

Common name: Emerald swallowtail
Species name: *Papilio palinurus*
Location: Southeast Asia

This is one of the very few green butterflies you can find in the world, and has a green band across both its wings. It flies very quickly, dashing in all directions.

Purple spotted swallowtail
Graphium weiskei

Blue diadem
Hypolimnas salmacis

Moduza nuydai (underside)

Blue morpho
Morpho rhetenor

Smaller wood nymph
Ideopsis gaura

Mylothris croceus

Cramer's blue butterfly
Morpho menelaus

Giant blue swallowtail
Papilio zalmoxis

Graphium swallowtail
Graphium androcles

Krishna peacock
Papilio krishna

Giant sulphur butterfly
Phoebis sennae

Prepona joiceyi

Great purple butterfly
Sasakia charonda

Taenaris selene

Orange beauty
Temenis laothoe

Rajah Brooke's birdwing
Troides brookiana

Extra stickers

Have fun sticking these anywhere.

Great orange tip butterfly
Hebemoia glaucippe

Red spot diadem butterfly
Hypolimnas usamara

Purple tip butterfly
Colotis ione

Emperor swallowtail
Papilio ophidicephalus

Monarch butterfly
Danaus plexippus

Clipper butterfly
Parthenos sylvia

Great mormon
Papilio memnon
(underside)

The sunset moth
Chrysiridia ripheus

Great eggfly butterfly
Hypolimnas bolina

Cornet moth
Argema mittrei

Queen Alexandra butterfly
Ornithoptera alexandrae

Indian moon moth
Actias selene

Blue morpho
Morpho cypris

Common lime or lemon butterfly
Papilio demodocus

Scarlet mormon butterfly
Papilio deiphobus (underside)

Green longwing
Philaethria dido

Golden birdwing
Ornithoptera croesus (underside)

Lacewing butterfly
Cethosia biblis

Emperor of India
Teinopalpus imperialis

Match the stickers

Peel off and stick the life-cycle stickers on pages 2 and 3,
and the butterfly stickers on pages 4 and 5.

Female lays egg

Caterpillar hatches

Caterpillar eats

Pupa changes

Caterpillar grows

Pupa

Sapphira butterfly
Asterope sapphira (female)

Butterfly

Orange tiger butterfly
Dryadula phaetusa

Citrus swallowtail
Papilio demoleus

Postman butterfly
Heliconius melpomeone

Blue mormon butterfly
Papilio polymnestor

Yariguies ringlet butterfly
Idioneurula donegani

American moon moth
Actias luna

Plain tiger butterfly
Danaus chrysippus

Emerald swallowtail
Papilio palinurus

Glasswing butterfly
Greta morgane oto

One-spotted prepona butterfly
Archaeoprepona demophon

Leaf butterfly
Kallima inachus

Rusty tipped page butterfly
Siproeta epaphus

Agrias butterfly
Agrias claudina

Sapho longwing
Heliconius sapho

Paper kite butterfly
Idea leuconoe

Blue wave butterfly
Myscelia cyaniris

Peleides blue morpho
Morpho peleides

Sara longwing
Heliconius sara

Atlas moth
Attacus atlas

Owl butterfly
Caligo beltrao

Schulze's agrias
Agrias claudia

Orange albatross butterfly
Appias nero

Blue mountain butterfly
Papilio ulysses

Asterope leprieuri

Sapphira butterfly
Asterope sapphira (male)

Bee butterfly
Chorinea sylphina

Esmeralda satyr
Cithaerias esmeralda

Malachite butterfly
Siproeta stelenes

Orange gull butterfly
Cepora aspasia

Buthan glory
Bhutanitis lidderdalii

Large salmon Arab
Colotis fausta

Magnificent forester
Euphaedra francina

Mocker swallowtail
Papilio dardanus

Blood-red cymothoe
Cymothoe sangaris

Common mapwing
Cyrestis thyodamas

Delias butterfly
Delias abrophora (underside)

Crenidomimas concordia

Euphaedra zampa

Tailed jay
Graphium agamemnon

Birdwing butterfly
Troides haliphron

Bronze duke butterfly
Euthalia nara

Blue butterfly
Arcas imperialis

South Indian blue oakleaf
Kallima horsfieldi

Doxocopa laurentia

Purple leaf butterfly
Fountainea nessus

Eighty-eight butterfly
Callicore pygas

Asterope markii

Paris peacock
Papilio paris

Memphis butterfly
Memphis glaucone

Hypolimnas pandarus

Common sailor
Neptis hylas

Greek shoemaker
Catonephele numilia

Striped blue crow
Euploea mulciber

Jungle jade butterfly
Papilio karna

Swallowtail butterfly
Heraclides thoas

Common green birdwing
Ornithoptera priamus

Clouded yellow butterfly
Colias croceus (underside)

Common name: Glasswing butterfly
Species name: *Greta morgane oto*
Location: Central America

This butterfly is called a glasswing because it has clear wings. It flies low in the forest between the bushes and plants.

Common name: One-spotted prepona butterfly
Species name: *Archaeoprepona demophon*
Location: Mexico to the Amazon

This turquoise and brown butterfly is a fast and strong flier and makes noises as it flies in the canopy. It feeds on rotten fruit and dung.

Common name: Blue wave butterfly
Species name: *Myscelia cyaniris*
Location: Texas. Mexico to Peru

The male of this blue and white butterfly perches on tree trunks along the forest edges.

Common name: Agrias butterfly
Species name: *Agrias claudina*
Location: Colombia to the Amazon

One of the most spectacular butterflies in the world. It is rarely seen as it flies high up in the forest canopy. It feeds on rotten fruits and mammal dung!

Common name: Rusty tipped page butterfly
Species name: *Siproeta epaphus*
Location: Mexico to the Amazon

The caterpillar has spiny, knobbed horns on its head. The orange adult flies in sunny open areas along forest edges and rivers.

Common name: Yariguies ringlet butterfly
Species name: *Idioneurula donegani*
Location: High mountains of Colombia

This butterfly only lives high in the mountains of Colombia, South America. It cannot be found anywhere else in the world.

Common name: Leaf butterfly
Species name: *Kallima inachus*
Location: Northern India, Vietnam, Cambodia, Laos

With its wings closed, the leaf butterfly looks like a dry leaf with dark veins. It is very well camouflaged in the jungle.

Common name: Sapho longwing
Species name: *Heliconius sapho*
Location: Central and northwestern South America

This butterfly only feeds on one host plant. It drinks the plant's poisons and they become part of its body, so it doesn't taste good to its predators. But the caterpillars can only eat the young leaves, because the mature leaves have too much poison in them.

Common name: Sara longwing
Species name: *Heliconius sara*
Location: Central and South America

This butterfly is found in open areas of lowlands in the tropical forest. The male mates with the female as soon as she emerges from the pupa.

Common name: Paper kite butterfly
Species name: *Idea leuconoe*
Location: Philippines and Borneo

This large white and black butterfly flies slowly. You can often see it in butterfly houses.

Common name: Peleides blue morpho
Species name: *Morpho peleides*
Location: Mexico to Colombia and Venezuela

This butterfly flies in a zig zag path along rivers, forest edges and through coffee plantations. It flies faster on sunny days.

Now for some fun!

Help the monarch butterfly find the nectar in the flower.
Use a pencil or a pen to draw a path through the maze.

▶ START

▶ FINISH

Can you spot the 5 differences between these two
emperor swallowtail butterflies?

Have you spotted that the pattern on one of a butterfly's wings is very often mirrored on the other wing? Colour the other wing of this butterfly.

You know all about the life-cycle of a butterfly now.
Put the letters in the correct order.

Your own garden

Use stickers or colour the butterflies to make your own butterfly garden.